Muscle Testing
Your Way To Health

OTHER BOOKS

Muscle Testing
Your Way To Health

by Using Emotions,
Nutrition, and Massage

by

BIOKINESIOLOGY
INSTITUTE

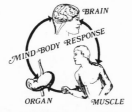

BIOKINESIOLOGY INSTITUTE

Written for Biokinesiology Institute, and assisted by the students of the 1980 and 1981 Biokinesiology Classes.

Special thanks for the diligent efforts of Alice and Steven Stroud, who assisted in the ideas, research, editing, and typing of this book.

Printed in the U. S. A.

ISBN 0-937216-07-0

For more information, contact:
BIOKINESIOLOGY INSTITUTE
461 Sawyer Road
Shady Cove, OR 97539
(503) 878-2398, or 878-2080

Note the list of other books written for your benefit by the authors on pages 106 and 107.

Production Coordination:
Michael Bass & Associates/P.O. Box 674/Ashland, OR 97520
Cover Design:
Lorena Laforest Bass

Contents

PART II HEALTH PROBLEMS

Introduction

WHAT IS HAPPENING TO HEALTH?

John Thie, in his book *Touch For Health*, well describes the dilemma of our modern health care systems: "The health care system in the United States and other western countries has developed to such an extent that the average person cannot successfully administer to the needs of his family, even for minor aches and pains, without resorting to the use of drugs. The system has increased to such a point of dependence, exploitation, and impotence that a great deal of frustration is being experienced by the people. When the public spends $5,200,000,000 for prescription drugs and another $2,200,000,000 for non-prescription drugs a year and they don't need two-thirds of them, it is time we take stock of what is going on in the health care field." What are some of our choices in today's health care system? Will any one of them give all the answers?

NUTRITION: This field covers foods, vitamins, minerals, herbs, homeopathics, etc. The herb and vitamin business would have you believe that everyone is being cured of any ailment under the sun, but the common people and the perplexed practitioner well realize that nutrition has its limitations. Part of the problem lies in the fact that "One Man's Food is Another Man's Poison." For example, the advice, "Take Vitamin C for Your Colds" is good for a few people, but our research has revealed that almost 50% of "cold" sufferers are allergic to vitamin C, in other words, vitamin C will do more harm than good for them. Just walk into a "Health Food Store" and note the hundreds of remedies; which one is for you? The guess-work of nutrition makes it most difficult for all of us. Something else is needed to assist us to find the right nutrition for each problem.

ALLEOPATHIC MEDICINE: Its case is well described previously by John Thie. Surgery and drugs seldom aid one to lasting health.

PSYCHIATRY: Some research by clear thinking women and men in this field has given us reason to consider possible connections between physical and emotional health. *The Encyclopedia Americana* (Vol. 18, p. 582b) states: "Since 1940 it has become more and more apparent that the physiologic function of organs and the organ systems are closely allied to the state of mind of the individual and that even tissue changes may occur in an organ so affected." Dr. J. E. Hett, in his book *Cancer,* gives us further reason to suspect a mind/body connection to health problems. He says: "The impulses of shock, worry, hatred, anger, jealousy, revenge and ill-will put extra pressure upon the endocrine glands. Through these, the functions of the stomach and intestines are inhibited. Poisons are created which do damage to the tissues. These, in turn, interfere with the proper activity of the mind. It becomes a vicious circle" (page 85).

Approximately in the year 716 BCE. King Solomon, using the highest authority of the universe as a guide, stated "A calm heart is the life of the fleshly organism, but jealousy is rottenness to the bones." Does this mean that psychiatry is the answer? No, but in its correct form it is a part of the whole.

MANUAL MANIPULATIONS: This is a very broad field that covers some very detailed sciences, such as Chiropracty, Acupuncture or Acupressure, Swedish Massage, Shiatsu, and

Rolfing, etc. The degree of success depends upon the problem. Many fine results have been seen in these fields because they often remove aggravating imbalances that cause illness. The shortcoming in these fields is that in themselves they do not necessarily consider nutritional imbalances nor emotional causes of illness. When properly applied, manual manipulations can be highly effective, safe, and an upbuilding part of the whole.

WHAT IS NEEDED?

UNITY! THE WHOLE IS GREATER THAN ITS PARTS! HEALTH COMES FROM THE WAY PEOPLE LIVE!

In this book we are trying to offer you the reader a glimpse, a foregleam of a method that you can use to find just what you need for your individual health problem. The prime tool for this method is muscle testing. We have tried to simply present muscle testing as a tool to measure the effectiveness of emotions, nutrition, and massage as they all interrelate to build up your health. Clearly we have not given you all of the "symptoms" nor "illnesses" that anyone may ever have, this would make the book far too complex. Also, there are so many varied therapies we could suggest, some being impractical for the beginner, that we have limited the suggested therapies to those that could easily and safely be done by you the reader. As you study this book we hope you will begin to see how to look at your problems as a whole picture of living, rather than "I caught a cold" or "My back just started aching."

The BIOKINESIOLOGY INSTITUTE is continuing its research on hundreds of different "symptoms" or illnesses, finding the crucial interconnections of Emotions, Nutrition and Physical Imbalances that often cause illness. As time permits we will be printing many more books designed to assist others to learn how to take care of themselves and others. About a dozen dedicated women and men scattered throughout the world are contributing directly to this work. The headquarters of the group is in Shady Cove, Oregon. If you desire more information about the field of Biokinesiology, please write or call the institute in Oregon, or your nearest practitioner. We would like to hear your experience in using this book—this will enable us to tailor future editions much more effectively.

Good health is a fleeting thing, keeping a balanced life with others in view, seeking peace and pursuing it, and demonstrating love toward others in all your affairs will assist you to live a longer, healthier and happier life.

John Barton

PART I
Methodology

Do you have an ache or pain? Where did it come from? Why is it there? Many people believe that pains are a God-given signal that there is a problem somewhere in your mind or body. This book is written for those people. Would you like to know why and where your problems may have come from and what you can intelligently do about them? Then carefully consider the many emotional-physical problems that are discussed in this book.

Where do problems come from? By far the great majority of our physical problems begin in the MIND, the BRAIN, the MARVELOUS COMPUTER, as it is led by the HEART. Let us consider a few examples. What happens to your stomach when you almost fall off a high ladder? Butterflies? Is that not a physical reaction caused by the emotion fear which originated in the mind? What happens to a young man's heart when he sees his girlfriend who has been gone for a few weeks? It beats rapidly. What happens if you feel angry and resentful as you eat a good meal? Your stomach begins to burn. Have you read the statement in the Bible, "Jealousy is rottenness to the bones" (Proverbs 14:30)? King Solomon, the compiler of the Proverbs, noted there was an emotional connection to health 2700 years ago. Where do problems come from? Again we state: FROM THE MIND AND HEART.

For the first time, the methods of self-healing which reach the deepest cause—one's emotions—have been put into a simple book form.

Specific problems have been included in this book to give you an opportunity to stimulate your mind and emotions in creative meditations. As you meditate upon the specific positive emotions, you may find that your pains will slowly melt away.

1

Creative meditations, which are easy to learn how to do, are highly effective if you have chosen the right ones. Just as the nutritional supplements will aid you to repair your body in a natural way, the creative meditations will rebuild your deepest emotional patterns in a natural manner.

The emotional exercises have been carefully chosen and prepared for simplicity by the authors and founders of the healing science called BIOKINESIOLOGY. This scientific field that unites the methods of creative meditation, nutritional supplementation, and exercise was established by using specialized muscle testing and high moral principles. The authors discovered that many of us actually already know the answers to our physical problems. Humans have incorporated many ideas and expressions that aid us in maintaining a degree of balance, such as:

1. "Don't eat when you're angry." Anger upsets the digestive system and can lead to massive maldigestion.

2. A person goes to his sick friend to "cheer him up" and he "feels better." The sick person is now a happy person, he feels better, his body gets a spurt of healing energy, and he has more strength.

3. Joggers claim that an emotionally sick person can get better if he jogs. Exercise stimulates the mind and body. Jogging can be an emotional stimulant.

4. The greatest commandments in the Bible are to "Love your Creator and your neighbor as yourself." Why? Because Love is the basic positive motivating force that helps us to live.

"Not only do all emotions (from the mind*) affect the heart, but there is also evidence that the* heart *in turn, affects the emotions."*
Aid to Bible Understanding,
The Watchtower Bible and Tract Society

How can we stimulate our health through positive emotions? By diligently studying about the emotional qualities found in the various programs and then applying them from your HEART through your MIND, you will find that your positive emotions begin to overrule your tiny negative spots. You and those around you will marvel at your changes. Those mountains that we made from molehills will disappear.

EMOTIONAL VITAMINS?

Many of us take vitamins and herbs, eat natural wholesome foods, and get a good amount of exercise to maintain our health. Now add to these beneficial steps an EMOTIONAL VITAMIN.

WHAT IS AN EMOTIONAL VITAMIN?

It is a capsule of good, living, balanced thinking. This is essential to a good preventive program. But just as very *specific* organic substances are needed to bring about bodily recuperation from a specific ailment, very specific emotions are needed to *repair* the body. Emotional vitamins give the body a boost in a precise area.

PACKING YOUR OWN EMOTIONAL VITAMINS?

In this book we have a specific packet of emotional thoughts tuned precisely for each of a variety of symptoms listed. You may use these ready-made emotional vitamins for problems that apply to you. In addition, we then teach you in this book how to pack your own emotional vitamins. You will learn how to pick the emotional ingredients that should be included in your personal "supplement."

EMOTIONAL VITAMINS—THE WINNERS!

One fine aspect of emotional vitamins is that you cannot HURT yourself by taking too much, whereas you might overdose on some organic substance or drug. There will be no warning labels on these vitamins. Another advantage is that if you take the "wrong" emotional vitamin for a specific problem, it won't hurt you! Do some more searching until you find an emotional vitamin that will help. One more asset for emotional vitamins is their cost. How much do you think such valuable aid will cost? Mental effort and heart-felt thought will be sufficient. We encourage you to give them a try! Pack your own emotional vitamin with the very *specific* emotions needed to *repair your body.*

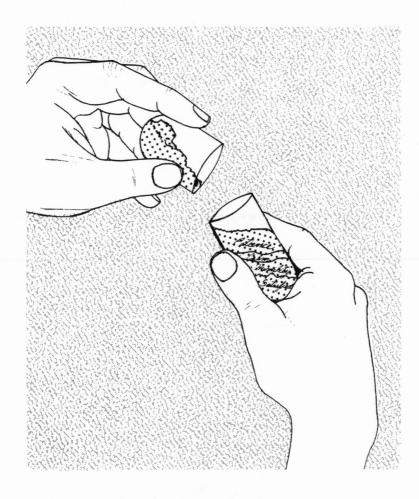

METHODS OF USING THIS BOOK

This book has been designed to be used in three different ways. The method you choose will depend on how much time you have, your interest and ability in muscle testing, and whether or not you have someone who can help you test.

FEEL IT—FIND IT!

Find the lesson which seems to correspond best to your problem and follow the instructions in the lesson. This method can be used with good results if you are alone or are unable to muscle test. (See page 7.)

TOUCH IT—TEST IT!

Touch testing is a method to help you to be sure that the lesson you have chosen is the correct one for you. (See page 8.)

EMOTION—TEST IT!

Once you have used some of the programs and are familiar with the methods, you may realize that you cannot find a lesson in the book which is exactly right for you. You can try Creative Emotion Testing yourself, or you can get instruction from Creative Health Instructors (Biokinesiologists). (See page 13.)

Look up your problem in the index. There may be several lessons listed. Turn to each of these lessons and read carefully the section called "PROBLEM." Find the lesson which seems to fit you the best. Remember that the symptoms listed are general so you may not have or be aware of all of them in yourself.

Work on your chosen lesson as described on pages 23 and 24. These lessons will work in most cases; however, they may not fit your particular situation. If you do not see results after a week of working faithfully on the program, you may wish to consult a Creative Health Instructor (Biokinesiologist).

EMOTIONS AND HEALTH

"In medical centers across the nation, evidence has been accumulating that grief, joy . . . affect our bodies far more than scientists have heretofore believed," reports an article in the New York Times *Magazine." Negative emotions are now seen as playing at least some role in "lowering a crucial threshold." Says the article: "Research indicates that anger and anxiety seem to play an important role in allowing the common herpes simplex virus to overpower the immune system, producing the ubiquitous canker sore."*

The article also reported on findings by Dr. Barbara Betz, who studied graduates of John Hopkins Medical School. Over a period of 30 years, she found that among those with good mental health and positive emotions, only about 25% suffered a heart attack or a bout with cancer. But for those who were moody and irritable, the number affected rose to 77%. "Your temperament and approach to life," she says, "certainly seem to have an effect on your resistance to disease."

Though some in the medical profession have been slow to discern the link between emotions and health, the Bible long ago made it clear, saying: "A heart that is joyful does good as a curer, but a spirit that is stricken makes the bones dry." Proverbs 17:22.

Watchtower, 4/1/81, pg. 15.

TOUCH IT—TEST IT!

Since the concept of touch testing may be difficult for some people to accept, the following is given as a brief explanation of how it works. For further information, see *How to Take Care of Yourselves Naturally* by the Biokinesiology Institute (John and Margaret Barton) or *Your Body Doesn't Lie* by John Diamond, M.D.

The mind (brain) is a self-sustaining electrically energized computer. It at all times tries to keep the body in proper balance—if there is an imbalance it will try to correct it. This process keeps us alive.

If there is a short circuit somewhere in the body, then there will be an imbalance in the electrical energy sent into that specific area. If you touch test that area using a strong arm, you will often find that the arm will weaken because the energy in the arm is drained into the weak area in an attempt to establish a balance. This causes a depletion of energy into that arm, and it will test weak.

"The likelihood is rather strong that MRT (Muscle Response Test) is effective because it operates on the energy pattern that exists on the surface of the body. The existence of this electrical field has been proven by Harold Burr, M.D. In the 1930's, Dr. Burr developed hypersensitive electronic instrumentation capable of reading electrical impulses in units as small as a millionth of a volt. Using this device, Burr discovered that there is considerable variation in the electrical charge present in different portions of a single body. He noted further that the voltage of the electrical charge varied greatly from day to day. Finally, he observed that different influences could change the electrical charge."

Muscle Response Test
by Dr. Walter Fischman and Dr. Mark Grinims

TESTING RULES FOR THE "TOUCH IT" TEST

1. Test in a room that is neutral in color (white, light, or brown) with no fluorescent lights.

2. Wear white or brown cotton clothing—no synthetic fabrics or metal (jewelry, belt buckles, glasses, etc.).

3. Keep the environment as quiet as possible. No interfering noises or music.

4. Neither person should have food in his or her mouth.

5. The person being tested must always face straight ahead while testing. Find a white or brown spot on the wall and fix the eyes on it.

6. The *palm* of the testor presses down on the *flexed wrist* of the testee.

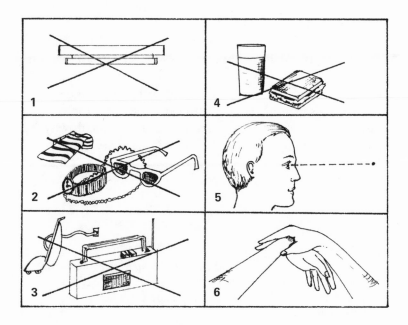

For more specific information on testing rules and variables, see the books *How to Take Care of Yourselves Naturally* or *Which Vitamin? Which Herb?* by the Biokinesiology Institute (John and Margaret Barton).

TESTING PROCEDURE FOR THE "TOUCH IT" TEST

1. **Before Beginning to Test**

   To be sure that your testing will be accurate, it is important that you and your friend work together as a loving, mild-mannered team. Always think "MILD" while testing —this will help your arm to respond properly. It is often helpful to meditate on the meaning of the word "MILD-NESS" for a few minutes before testing.

2. **Getting the "Feel" of Testing**

   Put the testee's right or left arm out straight horizontally (palm down), either to the front or to the side. Have the testor: 1) place his palm on the testee's flexed wrist (testee's hand hanging limp), 2) say "Hold," and 3) press down *gently* for about two seconds while the testee resists.

   Test several times to learn how gently strong the arm is. With the right amount of pressure and resistance, the arm will "lock" in place. (The art of this method is to *feel* the strength of the arm, not to break it!) Once you have this gentle baseline strength, be sure to use precisely the same pressure of resistance and downward thrust each time you test. You will need to *practice* this testing many times before you will get the "feel" of testing.

---

1. Before Beginning to Test . . . think MILDNESS

A MILD person is approachable and gracious. MILDNESS follows directly upon humility. A MILD-tempered person is not easily unbalanced or caused to lose his good sense. MILDNESS is important for one who is instructing another in order that his counsel will be well received.

ENEMIES OF MILDNESS are undue excitability, aggressiveness, a fighting attitude, haughtiness and highmindedness.

---

2. Getting the "feel" of Testing.

a. Palm on flexed wrist.

b. Say "hold."

c. Press down gently for about 2 seconds.

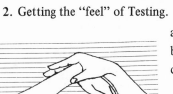

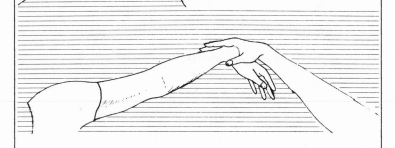

Determine baseline strength.
Arm will "lock" in place.

REMEMBER . . .

Too much resistance *or* too much downward thrust creates muscular strain.

PRACTICE is necessary to apply precisely the same pressure and downward thrust with each test.

PLATE A

3. Test the Touching Point in the Lesson.

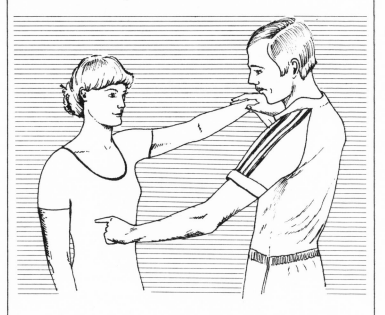

   a. Touch indicated location (bold dot) with fingertip(s) pointing directly into the body.
   b. Be sure to keep other fingers curled out of the way.
   c. Notice whether there is a slight difference in muscle strength.
   d. If slightly different, proceed to Step 4. If no difference, try another lesson.

PLATE B

4. Verify That You Have the Right Lesson

NUTRITIONAL VERIFICATION

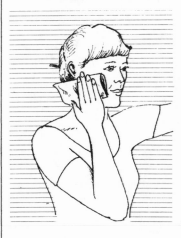

a. Hold nutrient on cheek at location of wisdom teeth (parotid gland).

b. Hold with palm side of fingers flat against your face.

c. Samples may be tested in clean, clear plastic bags.

d. Have your friend touch the weak point and retest your arm.

e. Repeat with each listed nutrient.

f. Is your arm stronger now?

EMOTIONAL VERIFICATION

a. Meditate on the specific positive emotions listed for about 20 seconds.

b. Retest the weak area to determine if you have strengthened it.

MASSAGE VERIFICATION

a. Massage the area indicated in the lesson.

b. Retest the weak point. If strong now, you have found a helpful lesson.

PLATE C

THE CAUSE OF ILLNESS*

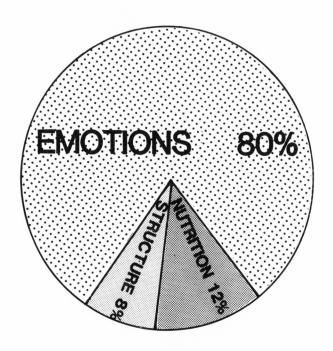

WHAT HAS TRIGGERED YOUR PROBLEM?

Did your illness come after a notable stress?
Did you get your illness from incorrect posture?
Were you eating just any old thing?

EMOTIONS–NUTRITION–STRUCTURE are all interconnected.
They are all part of the WHOLE!

*Due consideration needs to be given to 6,000 years of mankind's fall and resulting imperfection.

PLATE D

3. Test the Touching Point in the Lesson

Using the other hand, touch the indicated location, with the fingertip(s) pointing directly into the body (be sure to keep the other fingers curled out of the way). While touching this point, retest the arm, paying careful attention to notice whether there is a slight difference in muscle strength. Test the arm several times, both while touching and not touching the point. You may also need to move your fingers, testing different locations within the area indicated in the drawing (area is indicated by a bold ".".dot).

If there is a slight weakening when touching the point, proceed to step 4. If there is no difference, try a different lesson that involves the same problem. If you are unable to find one that tests weak, turn to the instructions for "Emotion Testing" (page 13), or consult a Biokinesiologist.

4. Verify That You Have the Right Lesson

At this point, you may simply go ahead and use the program given in the lesson. If you want to be sure that this is the right lesson for you, however, it is best to verify with nutrition, emotions, and massage.

NUTRITIONAL VERIFICATION

Using one or more of the nutritional suggestions given in the lesson, have your friend hold the nutrient on your cheek at the location of your wisdom teeth (this is the parotid gland, whose purpose is to signal your digestive system to prepare for the food which is in your mouth). The nutrient must be held with the *palm side of the fingers* flat against your face. Foods may be tested in clear plastic bags if necessary.

While your friend holds the nutrition to your cheek and you touch the weak point, retest the arm. If it is now stronger, you can assume that this nutrition is helpful in restoring balance in your body, and you probably have the correct lesson. It is best to verify this with all the listed nutrition, if you have them available. It is possible that not all of the nutrients will strengthen the imbalance because of your individual allergies. You may need to experiment to find your specific nutrition. Although this nutrition may help this particular weakness, it may not help other parts of your body. To be sure that the nutrition is good for your body *as a whole,* see the books *How to Take Care of Yourselves Naturally* or *Which Vitamin? Which Herb?* by the Biokinesiology Institute (John and Margaret Barton).

EMOTIONAL VERIFICATION

To be sure that the positive emotions given will help you with your problem, meditate briefly on these words for about 20 seconds, and then retest the weak area. If it is now strong, you know that developing these positive attitudes will be of value to you, both in balancing your physical problem and in improving your relationships with other people.

MASSAGE VERIFICATION

Retest the point. If it is still strong from your meditation, you will need to weaken it by saying, out loud, "Weak, weak, weak" while touching the point. Retest—it should once again be weak. Massage the muscle as indicated in the lesson. If you have the right lesson, the point should now test strong.

There will be times when the programs we have listed do not fit your problem. It will then be up to you to devise your own emotional program. Creative Emotion Testing is actually quite simple. The method of muscle testing is exactly the same as was described earlier:

1. Extend your arm to the side, have your friend gently press down on your wrist. Resist with the same firmness each time.

2. Touch a problem area (which will usually test weak) and retest. Your arm should weaken. If it does not, find another area that is weak or practice more. The key to accurate, successful muscle testing is FOLLOW THE RULES AND PRACTICE–PRACTICE–PRACTICE!

Now for EMOTION TESTING:

3. Touch the weak area (supposing that you are testing correctly) and then speak aloud several times each word from "A" to "T" (see page 14). Retest after saying each different word.

4. The word that makes your arm strong is the word that you need to use to frame your positive emotional correction.

5. Using the emotional word that made your weak arm strong, test its application. We will use the emotion "Cheerful" (lung) as an example:
You might say, "I need to be more cheerful" *Test:* Strong.
"I need to exercise more cheerfulness toward my wife" *Test:* Weak.
"I need to exercise more cheerfulness toward my son" *Test:* Strong.
"I need to exercise more cheerfulness toward my son when he is demanding my attention" *Test:* Strong.

13

6. I now meditate on how and why I need to pay more attention to my son, especially when he is demanding my attention. For an added impact on the brain I can touch the top of my head with my fingertips while audibly talking to myself about being more cheerful.

The above explanation has been simplified for the usage of the reader of this book. Creative emotion testing can become quite involved and ought to be done with great care, thoughtfulness, love, tactfulness, and high morality.

EMOTION RELATED ORGAN

	EMOTION	RELATED ORGAN
A	HUMBLE	GALLBLADDER
B	CHEERFUL	LUNG
C	COMMUNICATIVE	PINEAL
D	CALM	THUMUS
E	SECURE	HEART
F	SUCCESSFUL	EYE
G	RELIABLE	STOMACH
H	SUPPORTIVE	EAR
I	JOYFUL	PAROTID, SPLEEN, PITUITARY
J	ASSURED	URINARY BLADDER
K	APPROVED	PANCREAS
L	SERVING	THYROID
M	CONTENT	LIVER
N	PLEASANT	HYPOTHALAMUS
O	HARMONIOUS	SKIN
P	APPRECIATED	SMALL INTESTINES
Q	MERCY	LARGE INTESTINES
R	SATISFIED	REPRODUCTIVE ORGANS
S	STEADFAST	KIDNEY
T	PEACEFUL	ADRENALS, PARATHYROID

CONGRATULATIONS!

You have now learned what positive emotions and nutrition your body needs in order to restore balance. In a sense, this is the easy part. What is often more difficult is to actually apply the emotions in your daily life and to bring about a definite, long-lasting change in the way you feel and act toward your fellow humans and your life.

"My own mouth will speak things of wisdom, And the meditation of my heart will be of things of understanding."

Psalms 49:3

HOW TO TAKE AN EMOTIONAL BALANCING VITAMIN

The use of ACTIVE MEDITATION—which means meditating, concentrating, and mulling over in your mind specific positive information in an audible undertone—has been found to be one of the most useful methods for correcting emotional problems. The method is simple, yet very difficult for most of us to do. The difficulty is that the world we live in seldom teaches us how to think and see things in a positive, upbuilding way. In order to overcome the negativity, try to find good and joyful things to think about and share with others each day.

How can you implant positive emotions into your beautiful brain, especially the specific emotions that you may need in order to overcome some emotional problem that has brought about a physical manifestation? Follow the steps indicated below.

1. Hold the top of your head (the emotional input point—see diagram) with the fingers pointing down toward the middle of your brain. This will cause a slight enhancement of your brain's ability to hear and remember the emotions that you are going to discuss (if this technique feels uncomfortable, OMIT, however, it can be beneficial).

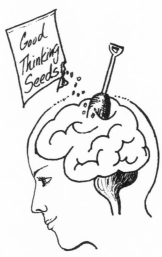

2. Concentrate upon your specific positive emotional program, considering the meaning of each of the key words. How can you apply them to your daily life? What do they actually mean? Dig deep into the heart motivation. Do all of this *audibly*—"talking to yourself" in an undertone.

   You may need some assistance in doing this active meditation. Ask a loving friend to help you. This may assist you in determining toward whom or in what situations you may need to focus your good thoughts for the day.

   Next, you may need to use some high quality reference books to help you to understand the scope of meaning of some of the positive emotional words in your program.

3. ACT upon your positive emotions! Demonstrate the needed emotions from your heart.

4. Repeat your active meditations 3 or 4 times per day for about 1 to 2 minutes each time. The severity of your physical manifestation (your health problem) and the speed with which you are able to regain your balance of health will determine the amount of time to spend on your EMOTIONAL VITAMIN program. The variables here could mean anywhere from one time to several years. Taking the suggested food supplements and massaging the suggested areas assist the emotional correction.

Work hard, and with patience. It often takes years of bad living habits to destroy good health; it may take real effort to regain the balance of health that you desire.

I have a splitting headache which seems to be localized on the sides of my head. Also, there is a tenderness at the back of my neck and in my tailbone area. I just ate some yogurt and now I feel queasy in my stomach. Turning to the index, I look under "headache" and notice that there are several kinds listed. Forehead? No, that's not my problem. Temporal? That looks right! I turn to lesson #33 and read the list of problems. I don't know about the allergies, but just the thought of eating those foods sounds bad to me—and I really do have a pain in the front of my temples!

My wife and I test my arm. She pushes gently on my wrist and it is strong. Then I touch the point indicated on the drawing (on me) with my fingertip and she retests my arm—it is clearly weaker. This is another direct proof that there is a problem in my temples. While I continue to touch the weak point on my temple, my wife holds the suggested nutrition on my cheek, and we test again. Lo and behold my arm stays up strong! This is the right nutrition.

Now I earnestly try to meditate on the positive thoughts of peacefulness and gratefulness. It is easy for me to see where the problem came from, so I next sit down with my wife and apologize to her for causing a problem earlier in the day. Now I meditate again with a clear conscience.

Next, my wife helps me retest the point which is now strong, but the headache is still there! I remember reading about the importance of repetition (page 17)—that it will take time, effort, and repetition to relieve the problem. Several hours later my wife asks me how I feel. "Fine!" Yes, my problem just gently disappeared without me even knowing it!

Miss J, who is a young, healthy woman, is a little quiet and reserved. She often smiles and wishes to take an active part in many things, but a physical problem will suppress her participation. One day Miss J was conversing with some people at a health gathering. On the surface, to a bystander, all appeared well, but she commented that she "had to sit down." Her fiance, Mr. H, gave a hopeless look and said, "She has hypoglycemia" (low blood sugar). A friend who was with them suggested, "Let's test it and find out what happened." Mr. H, knowing what testing might do to help her, was eager to try. The two of them tested the point indicated on page 64. Mr. H's strong arm FLOPPED down, totally losing strength, to the couple's gasping amazement. (Mr. H is a very husky man.) They had seen testing done, but had never experienced the real feel of it. They were on the right point!

It was rapidly found that FAITH and SUCCESSFUL strengthened the point mentioned. The problem centered upon using FAITH and SUCCESS toward those that did not agree with Miss J's viewpoint on health. (This is a very common problem among holistic, health-oriented individuals.)

The couple talked about the positive emotions while holding the EMOTIONAL INPUT point on Miss J's head. Mr. H and the friend then turned their attention to other topics while Miss J rested for just a moment. Miss J came over and began to participate actively in the discussion. It was soon noted that she was acting very lively. "How do you feel?" "Fine! Was that all I needed to do to get rid of my weakness?" Miss J was a changed person! A few hours later she was seen scurrying about, visiting with many people. A wonderful new step had come into her life.

Yes, emotions can and do control a very large part of our health and life. Miss J's problem was simple, yet oh so common. Some problems will be solved this easily—yet remember, some will take a firm effort over a lengthy period.

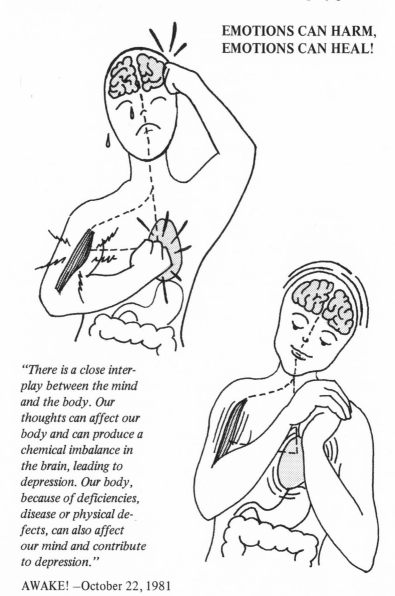

EMOTIONS CAN HARM, EMOTIONS CAN HEAL!

"There is a close interplay between the mind and the body. Our thoughts can affect our body and can produce a chemical imbalance in the brain, leading to depression. Our body, because of deficiencies, disease or physical defects, can also affect our mind and contribute to depression."

AWAKE! —October 22, 1981

STRAINING AT THE BONDS OF NATURAL AFFECTION

We are looking at a normally happy family group, a loving husband and wife and their delightful 2-year-old girl. They really enjoy one another's company, but sometimes there are strains on that bond of natural affection. For example, the little nursing one is overly demanding for several nights in a row, leaving almost no time for the husband and wife to get together and hold one another. They still realize intellectually, of course, that they love one another and that this breech between them was necessary, but the husband feels in his heart unhappy and disappointed, just a little left out.

The next day he really isn't so communicative with his wife; he appears a bit tense and doesn't admire or caress her as he usually does. The wife notices this and feels that her husband isn't attracted to her; she feels somehow repulsive in his eyes.

That evening when the little one goes to sleep, the husband and wife hold one another, but something is not quite right. The wife doesn't respond with as much tenderness, although she tries to, knowing her husband needs her affections.

She complains of a raw, sore throat. They test the throat and find that the emotion is a feeling of foolishness and repulsiveness and that makes her allergic to the bed foam. This allergy passes through the mother's milk, so it in turn causes the baby to be restless and cranky as she lies in bed sleeping.

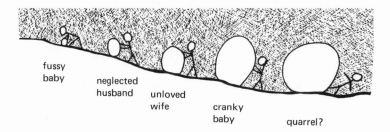

fussy
baby   neglected
husband   unloved
wife   cranky
baby   quarrel?

Do you see how this situation is rapidly snowballing? Now the upset mother will have to spend the rest of the night nursing and putting the baby back to sleep—and do you picture the husband rolling over and grumbling?

Yes, our petty emotions can certainly strain the bonds of natural affection, and don't we all have a little of that selfish bent, where we put our own needs first, waiting for others to love us first before we respond with love.

Now can you see the use of guarding our emotions— becoming aware of what they do to us? Thinking about how we feel could save a quarrel or two!

Many persons do not realize that the cause of their pains may be emotional, reports Rene Cailliet, M.D., professor and chairman of rehabilitation medicine at the University of Southern California, Dr. Cailliet believes that people are spending millions of dollars trying to relieve pain symptoms that are actually caused by unpleasant relationships. "Sometimes the tension is manifested in strain on the muscles of the neck. Some victims suffer the same tension pain in the back. Others get peptic ulcers, migraines or heart attacks. Still others experience pain in one place, then another, or in various places simultaneously." He observes that such cases are difficult to diagnose and adds: "Many patients are averse to admitting that their pain is caused by on-the-job or home-related anger, anxiety or depression. They'd rather blame their pain on an old or imagined injury."

"Watching the World"
AWAKE! —December 22, 1981

EXPLANATION OF LESSONS

Each lesson has five parts to it:

1. **PROBLEM**: A generalized list of problems associated with the mind-body imbalance is given. You may notice all, or perhaps only a few of these in yourself. The "symptoms" given are not to be used as a diagnostic tool, but if your doctor tells you that you have these symptoms, you may look them up for your own education and enjoyment. We are not teaching you how to treat medical symptoms, but how to view the mind-body energy balance in its positive aspects.

2. **EMOTIONAL VITAMIN**: This is a precise list of several words that are key emotions controlling specific functioning systems within your body. It is important to meditate on these words and incorporate them into your life. Think about how you can apply them to specific areas in your persent life. The meditation should be done for one to five minutes, three times per day (if your problem is difficult) for as long as the problem persists. Make these emotions a part of your life.

3. **NUTRITION**: This is a list of a few foods, vitamins, herbs, and cell salts that have been found useful to encourage the mind and body to generate better healing energies for the particular problem listed. Dosage will depend upon your wisdom, the recommended dosage of the manufacturer, and your legal doctor.

4. **CAUSE**: We are concerned not with the medical reason for a problem, but rather what is happening to the body-mind energy balance.

5. **MASSAGE**: The addition of massage to this book is to assist you in becoming aware of physical stresses and how they relate to emotional and nutritional imbalances. Massage is normally done for 2 to 5 minutes on large areas, or 30 seconds on small areas and continued until the area is no longer tender. This will frequently mean 2 to 3 times a day for 2 to 4 weeks. For further information on assisting muscular and structural balance, see *Be Your Own Chiropractor*, by the Biokinesiology Institute (John and Margaret Barton).

Research has shown that our thinking can affect our brain chemistry. For example, during a 1979 study some dental patients had their wisdom teeth extracted and were given a salt solution by injection, a placebo, and were told that this would ease the pain. Although this had no actual pain killing ability, reportedly one third stated that their pain was dramatically reduced. It is thought that naturally occurring "pain killers" (endorphins) of the brain were put to work by the person's thoughts. This was later verified when another drug was administered to block the effects of the brain's natural "pain killers" and the pain returned.

"The power of the mind to respond to love has been seen in numerous cases. Conversely, anger, hatred, jealousy and other negative emotions also have been found to produce biochemical changes in the body."

AWAKE! —September 8, 1981

PART II

Health Problems

PROBLEM: Pains in ascending and descending colon below navel, also some small intestine cramping below navel.

EMOTIONAL VITAMIN: *KINDNESS, SATISFIED*

NUTRITION: E complex (with selenium and chromium), Dr. Christopher's formula "Barberry LG," mustard greens, rice polish.

CAUSE: A spasming of the peristaltic muscles in the lower abdomen. This is related to an adrenal imbalance.

MASSAGE each tender area deeply and gently for one minute.

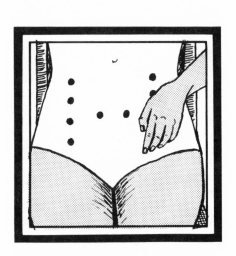 

PROBLEM: Spasms of transverse colon pain in the upper abdominal area going across the body about 3 to 4 fingers width above the navel.

EMOTIONAL VITAMIN: *FAITH, SATISFIED*

NUTRITION: Magnesium.

CAUSE: A spasming of the peristaltic muscles of the transverse colon, each set (about ½" wide) becoming periodically weak and then overstressed (very tense). This is related to an adrenal imbalance.

MASSAGE deeply in small circles for one minute at each location.

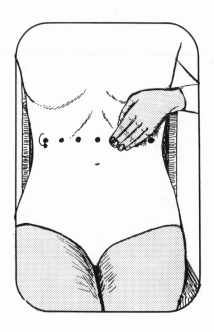

PROBLEM: Weakness, anemia. Low back ache. Allergy to iron in foods.

EMOTIONAL VITAMIN: *SELF-CONTROL, PATIENT.*

NUTRITION: C complex with bioflavonoids and rutin, orange peels, soy protein powder, homeopathic "Nerve."

CAUSE: An emotional imbalance of thymus, adrenals, and stomach, creating an allergy to (an inability to assimilate) iron in foods.

MASSAGE up back of neck.

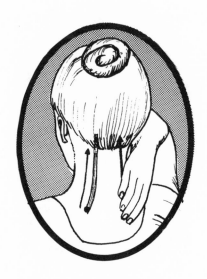

PROBLEM: Bedwetting. Poor bladder control. Sore eyebrows. External vaginal irritation. Second pre-molar lower tender.

EMOTIONAL VITAMIN: *KINDNESS, AGREEABLE.*

NUTRITION: B-2, B-3 (niacin), herbal diuretic, kelp, lecithin, mineral complex, papaya.

CAUSE: A mal-signal and nerve irritation to the first bladder control valve (sphincter muscle in the urethra).

MASSAGE on midline from pubic bone up toward navel.

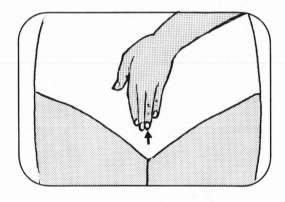

PROBLEM: Poor bladder control. Bedwetting.

EMOTIONAL VITAMIN: *SELF-CONTROL, ACCEPTED.*

NUTRITION: F (linoleic and linoletic acid), lecithin, bio-chemic phosphates, calc flour, kali phos, nat sulph.

CAUSE: A mal-signal and nerve irritation to the third (outer) bladder control valve (the sphincter muscle in the urethra).

MASSAGE up and toward ear on back of neck.

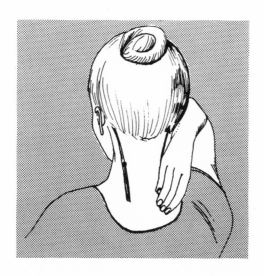

PROBLEM: Bloating. Diaper rash on folds of groin. Sore intestines. Canine tooth sensitivity.

EMOTIONAL VITAMIN: *MILDNESS, HELPFUL.*

NUTRITION: PABA, nerve, slippery elm.

CAUSE: An imbalanced nerve energy going to the small intestines, causing poor digestion and bloating. This same nerve pathway goes to the groin area near the folds of the hip and leg. At this location one could find skin sensitivity or even a rash.

MASSAGE down the lower half of the upper arm (front side) and the upper fourth of the front of the lower arm.

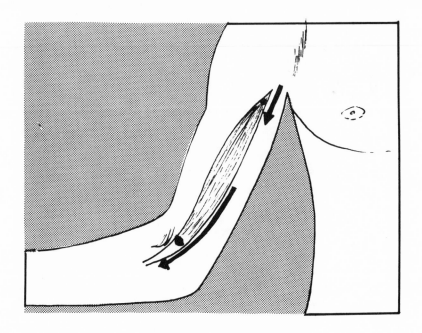

PROBLEM: Blood pressure is too high or too low. Stiff back. Difficulty in touching toes.

EMOTIONAL VITAMIN: *FAITH, YIELDING.*

NUTRITION: B-6, B-12, E, F, kelp, lecithin, mineral complex, postassium-iodine, protein powder, zinc, cayenne, ginger, honey, columbine, papaya seed, red clover, yucca.

CAUSE: Imbalance in the Posterior Pituitary hormone secretion, causing too much or not enough fluid in blood.

MASSAGE at base of spine by pressing in deeply between spine and hip bone.

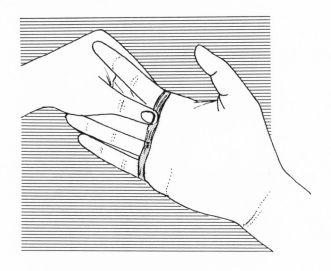

PROBLEM: High or low blood pressure.

EMOTIONAL VITAMIN: *FAITH, YIELDING.*

NUTRITION: B-6, B-12, E complex, kelp, zinc, lecithin, mineral complex, soy protein powder, potassium-iodine, cayenne, ginger, honey, papaya seeds, red clover, yucca.

CAUSE: Imbalance in the Posterior Pituitary hormone secretion, causing too much or not enough fluid in the blood.

MASSAGE up the upper back to the middle of the neck.

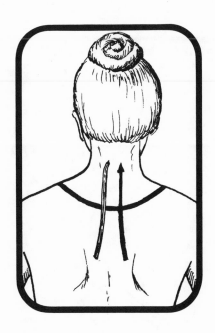

PROBLEM: "Cold" syndrome. Deep bronchial cough. Pain in elbow joint.

EMOTIONAL VITAMIN: *FAITH, ACCEPTED.*

NUTRITION. Potassium-iodine, nat sulph, soy protein powder.

CAUSE: A nerve response to the little ciliary hairs in the bronchial tubes, which normally push mucus up and out, is malfunctioning, causing the mucus to go down the tubes —therefore the need for coughing.

MASSAGE down the lower end of the upper arm and ¼ of the way down the front of the lower arm (deeply).

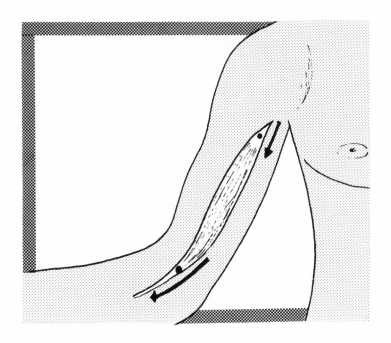

PROBLEM: Bruising easily. Hemorrhoids. Sore gums. Varicose veins.

EMOTIONAL VITAMIN: *GOODNESS, UNDERSTANDABLE.*

NUTRITION: C complex with bioflavonoids and rutin, mineral complex, horsetail, strawberry leaves.

CAUSE: The blood supply to a section of the liver and pancreas is stagnating, causing the liver to fail to produce the proper nutrients to keep the walls of the blood vessels and capillaries strong. This predisposes one to injury and rupture to the blood vessels.

MASSAGE down the front of the forearm.

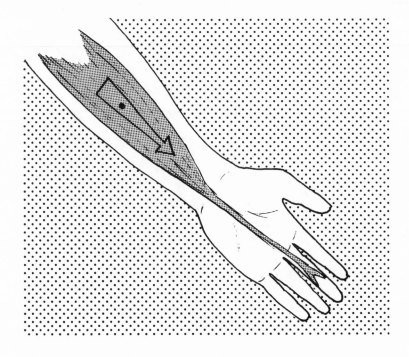

#11 BRUISING EASILY

PROBLEM: Bruising easily. Tendency to have varicose veins, hemorrhoids, and sore gums.

EMOTIONAL VITAMIN: *FAITH, ACCEPTED.*

NUTRITION: A, B-12, C complex (including rutin and bioflavonoids), E complex, lecithin, mineral complex, pancreatin complex, vegetable laxative, colic, horsetail, strawberry leaves.

CAUSE: Imbalance of a special functioning between the pancreas, spleen, kidney, and liver, causing weak capillary walls and predisposing one to bruising, hemorrhoids and varicose veins.

MASSAGE deeply down the front of your lower arm (see problem #10) and up the side of your neck.

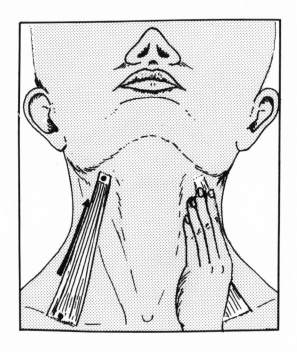

PROBLEM: Dry, chapped lips.

EMOTIONAL VITAMIN: *GOODNESS, WILLING.*

NUTRITION. E complex, PABA, mitrewort, ponderosa needles.

CAUSE: An insufficient supply of lymph to the thymus and lips causing poor skin growth on the lips (dry lips).

MASSAGE deeply up front of neck to the sides of the Adam's apple, and on the chest from the breastbone to the shoulders.

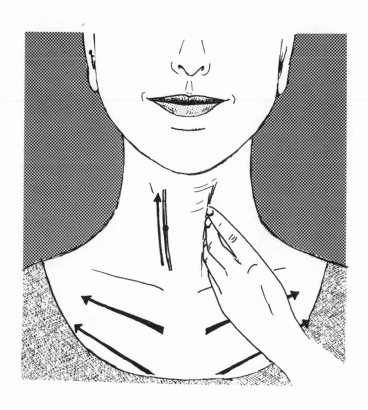

PROBLEM: Runny, congested nose. Possible skin rash on back of forearm below elbow. Sore bone on outside of foot. Allergy to polyester and foam rubber.

EMOTIONAL VITAMIN: *SELF-CONTROL, COMFORT-ABLE.*

NUTRITION: B-6, comfrey-pepsin, iron, zinc, lecithin, magnesium, potassium-iodine, ferrum phos, kali phos, silicea.

CAUSE: The runny nose is the body's way of attempting to counteract the irritation from plastics, which it cannot do because of the emotional imbalance.

MASSAGE down the outside of your upper arm and on the thumb side of the front of your lower arm to the wrist.

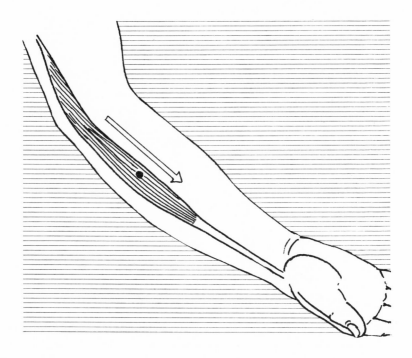

PROBLEM: Cradle cap near top center of head. Allergy to most green vegetables and herbs (especially wheat grass, alfalfa sprouts, and comfrey).

EMOTIONAL VITAMIN: *KINDNESS, COMFORTED.*

NUTRITION: EPG, mineral complex, magnesium, homeopathic teething compound, calc sulph, kali phos.

CAUSE: An imbalance of energy between the thymus and adrenals, causing unhealthy skin growth on the top of the head.

MASSAGE bottom of foot from heel to third toe.

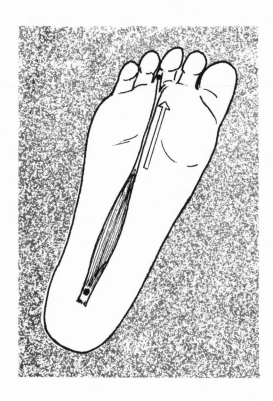

PROBLEM. Cradle cap on top of head. Pain inside hip cavity, difficulty in walking. Diaper rash. Allergy to carrots, eggs, cheese, honey, yeast, B-1, B-2.

EMOTIONAL VITAMIN: *KINDNESS, INCLUDED.*

NUTRITION. Digestive Complex (HCL), mineral complex, catnip, cayenne.

CAUSE: Hormonal imbalance, causing improper absorption of nutrition in intestines and poor growth of skin on top of the head.

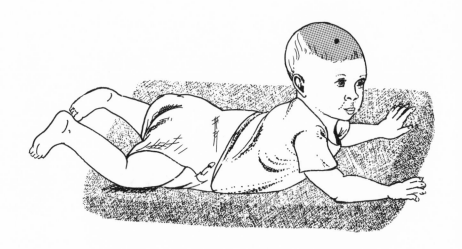

PROBLEM: Dandruff above and behind the ear. Itchy scalp.

EMOTIONAL VITAMIN: *LONG-SUFFERING, USEFUL.*

NUTRITION: B-6, lecithin, mineral complex.

CAUSE: A lack of blood supply to the scalp in this area causes unhealthy skin and therefore dandruff.

MASSAGE any sore areas on the chin, gently.

PROBLEM: Dizziness when standing up. Possible hypoglycemia.

EMOTIONAL VITAMIN: *MILDNESS, ACCEPTING.*

NUTRITION: B-6, B-12.

CAUSE: Adrenal insufficiency causing low blood pressure, especially to the head when getting up.

MASSAGE up on lower front of the neck.

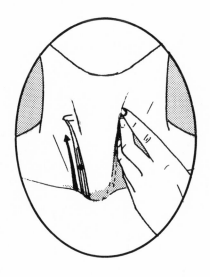

PROBLEM: Dry, irritated eyelids. Low back pains. Gas. Allergy to yeast, B Complex, PABA.

EMOTIONAL VITAMIN: *SELF-CONTROL, RESPECTED.*

NUTRITION: B-6, calcium, mag phos, aloe vera, apple cider vinegar.

CAUSE: A nerve supply to the mucus lining of the eyelid is being interrupted here. Also, the emotions to the stomach and intestines cause an imbalance in the ability to use the allergens.

MASSAGE very deeply up and in from the pelvis (hips) to the lower spine.

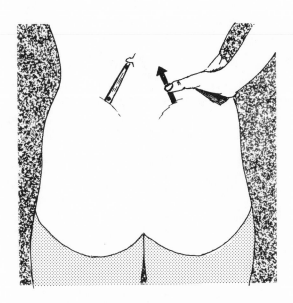

PROBLEM: Earache.

EMOTIONAL VITAMIN: *PEACE, TRANQUIL.*

CAUSE: Interference in the blood and hormone supply to the ear, causing tenderness and pains.

MASSAGE the sole of the foot from the heel to the toes.

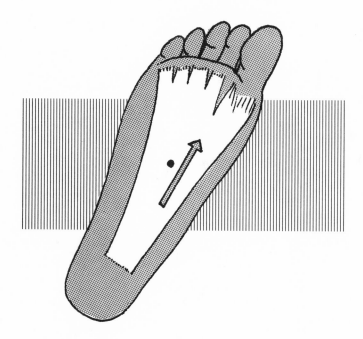

PROBLEM: Gas, bloating. Sore breast. Allergy to wheat, rye, barley, rice, eggs, alfalfa.

EMOTIONAL VITAMIN: *PEACE, JOYFUL, GRATEFUL.*

NUTRITION: B-6, F (linoleic acid), pancreatin complex, soy protein powder.

CAUSE: A lack of pancreas enzymes causes a series of allergies and the accompanying gas and bloating from mal-digestion.

MASSAGE across the bottom of the ball of the foot very deeply.

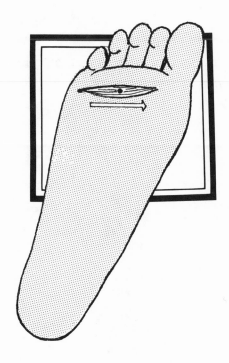

PROBLEM: Gas (flatulence). Poor digestion. Psoriasis. Non-malignant tumors. Allergies to soybeans, soy products (tofu, protein powders, etc.), nuts, and possibly milk products.

EMOTIONAL VITAMIN: *KINDNESS, LISTENING.*

NUTRITION: A, B-6, C complex with rutin and bioflavonoids, digestive compound with HCL, E complex with selenium and chromium, garlic and parsley, lecithin, mineral complex, pancreatin complex, changease (Dr. Christopher formula), ferrum phos, kali phos, silicea, apple cider vinegar, apricots and kernels, asparagus, grapefruit, grapes, figs, cabbage, sweet potato, papaya, cinnamon, comfrey and pepsin, plain yogurt.

CAUSE: Imbalance of hormones for digestion and tissue growth.

MASSAGE down outside and back of lower leg.

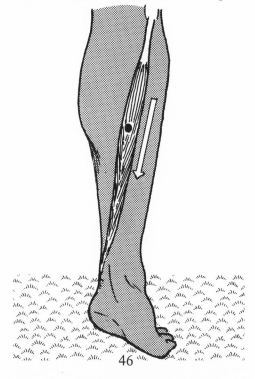

PROBLEM: Gas (flatulence). Abnormal tissue. "Worry-wart."

EMOTIONAL VITAMIN: *KINDNESS, THOUGHTFUL.*

NUTRITION: A, B-6, C complex with rutin and bioflavonoids, digestive compound with HCL, E complex with selenium and chromium, garlic and parsley, lecithin, mineral complex, pancreatin complex, changease (Dr. Christopher's formula), ferrum phos, kali phos, silicea, apple cider vinegar, apricots and kernels, asparagus, grapefruit, grapes, figs, cabbage, sweet potato, papaya, cinnamon, comfrey and pepsin, plain yogurt, soy protein powder.

CAUSE: Imbalance of tissue growth in the body due to imbalanced hormone reaction between the pancreas and reproductive organs.

MASSAGE down outside and back of lower leg.

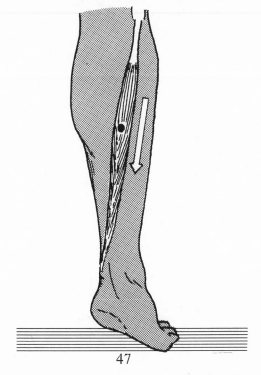

PROBLEM: General tendency to get headaches. Large intestines malfunctioning. One of the contributing causes of multiple sclerosis. Upper second molar tender. Allergy to garlic, rice, radishes, vitamin F.

EMOTIONAL VITAMIN: *FAITH, UNITED.*

NUTRITION: B-3 (niacin), mineral complex, pancreatin complex, potassium-iodine.

CAUSE: Each square inch of the large intestine is responsible for assimilating specific nutrients. Any one area malfunctioning will cause an imbalance in some specific nutrient. This chain-reaction can set off many "illnesses," from headaches to multiple sclerosis, and anything in between.

MASSAGE firmly down sides of both legs for three minutes.

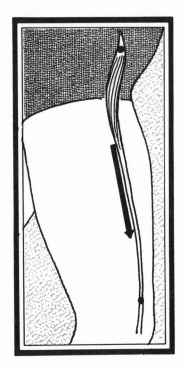

PROBLEM: General tendency to get headaches. Achy all over. Nauseated. Allergy to B-5 (pantothenic acid), tomatoes, coconut, cantaloupe.

EMOTIONAL VITAMIN: *FAITH, SATISFIED.*

NUTRITION: C complex, mineral complex, honey, willow bark and leaves.

CAUSE: Restricted blood flow to head, causing a predisposition to headaches.

MASSAGE up upper back between shoulder blades.

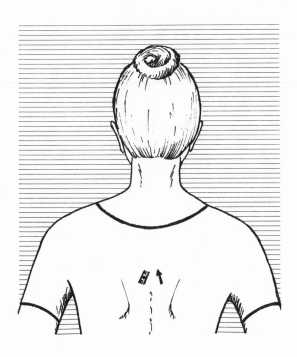

PROBLEM: Headache behind eyes. Itchy scalp. Allergy to polyvinylchloride and foam rubber (mattresses). Runny nose.

EMOTIONAL VITAMIN: *PEACE, YIELDING.*

NUTRITION: A, B complex, B-12, kali phos, mag phos.

CAUSE: This type of headache is caused by a lack of blood flow to a small bone under the bridge of the nose (vomer) and therefore

MASSAGE up along the front of the neck very deeply and carefully.

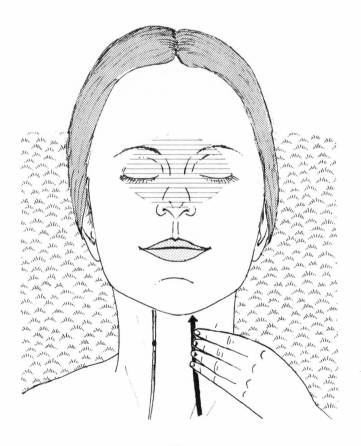

PROBLEM: Frontal headache. Sore, stiff upper shoulder. Allergy to A, E, F, soy products.

EMOTIONAL VITAMIN: *KIND, SUCCESSFUL.*

NUTRITION: Iron, mineral complex, pancreatin, nat sulph, kali mur, kali phos.

CAUSE: An insufficient flow and stagnation of blood to the forehead area.

MASSAGE up back sides of neck firmly and from shoulders to back of head.

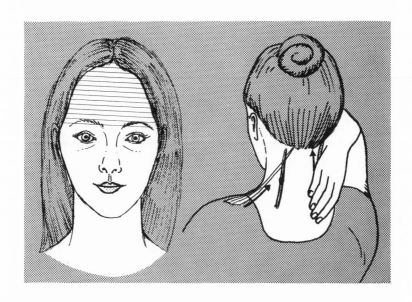

PROBLEM: Deep frontal "sinus" headache. Skin rash on sternum. Pain in upper back of neck. Allergy to sage, honey, pancreatin.

EMOTIONAL VITAMIN: *SELF-CONTROL, RESPONSIBLE.*

NUTRITION: B complex, protein powder, protein tablets, pre-natal tea, bay leaf, brewer's yeast, licorice, milkweed.

CAUSE: Lack of blood supply to deep area behind eyes (ethmoid bone). Can also be caused by metal in front pockets.

MASSAGE up under base of skull.

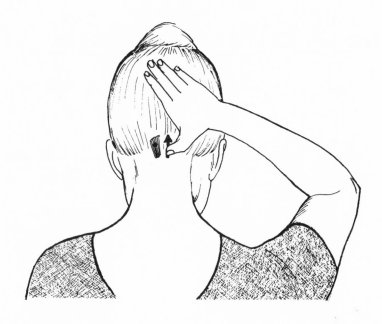

PROBLEM: Headache around the head at about the area a hat sits on the head. Allergy to foam rubber.

EMOTIONAL VITAMIN: *SELF-CONTROL, REMEMBERING.*

NUTRITION: Pancreatin complex, Standard's #38 homeopathic preparation.

CAUSE: This nerve to blood system reaction sets off a chain that involves parts of the thymus, spleen, pineal, and kidney. It restricts blood flow to a portion of the skull.

MASSAGE cheeks toward the mouth; and from the wrist to the thumb, on the palm side.

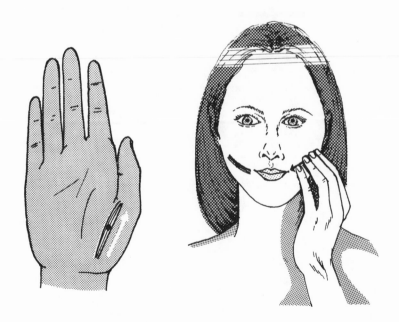

PROBLEM: Headache in inner eye socket area, under bridge of nose. Diaper rash. Skin irritation on crown of head.

EMOTIONAL VITAMIN: *FAITH, WILLING.*

NUTRITION: B-3 (niacin), lecithin, pancreatin, silicea, chicory root.

CAUSE: Restriction of blood flow to the area of deep inner eye socket (lacrimal bone).

MASSAGE up front side of neck.

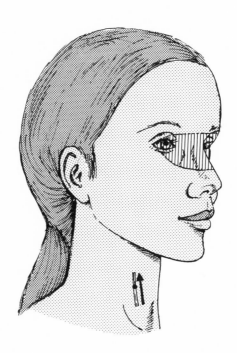

PROBLEM: Headache in "sinus" area below eyes (actually it is in the deep cheek tissue). Tender first molar (lower).

EMOTIONAL VITAMIN: *FAITHFULNESS, ADAPTABLE.*

NUTRITION: Potassium-iodine, kali sulph.

CAUSE: A stagnation of lymph fluid in the sinus and deep cheek area, causing a build-up of toxins.

MASSAGE up on front side of neck.

PROBLEM: Headache in the temples. Upper neck pains.

EMOTIONAL VITAMIN: *HOPE, FRIENDLY.*

NUTRITION: B-3 (niacin), potassium-iodine.

CAUSE: Congestion in the large intestines, causing a restriction of blood flow into the temple area (temporalis bone) and therefore the painful accumulation of toxins in the head.

MASSAGE down on the temple area, especially in the area above the ear.

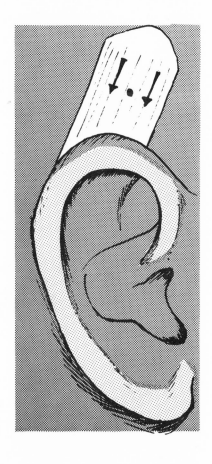

PROBLEM. Headache in the temple area. Tailbone pains. Allergy to alfalfa, comfrey, kelp, milk products. Gas.

EMOTIONAL VITAMIN: *SELF-CONTROL, OBSERVANT.*

NUTRITION: B-1, digestive complex with HCL, E complex, lecithin.

CAUSE: This mild tenderness in the temples is caused by a nerve malfunction going to the temple bone. This same nerve goes to the stomach and thymus, causing them not to properly accept the noted "allergic" foods.

MASSAGE down on your tailbone area.

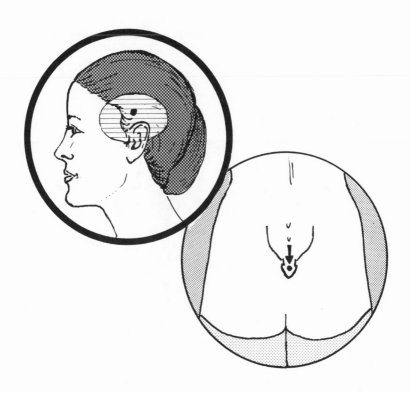

PROBLEM: Headache in the temporal area. Headache or tenderness in the back of the head. Pain in the tailbone or sacral area. Pain during intercourse. Runny nose. Gas. Allergy to grains, legumes, protein, yogurt, cheese, nuts, carrots, cabbage, broccoli, iron, garlic-parsley.

EMOTIONAL VITAMIN: *PEACE, GRATEFULNESS.*

NUTRITION: E, zinc, arnica, nat sulph, ponderosa needles, bracken fern.

CAUSE: One unusual cause is that this specific nerve-tendon supply is often damaged during birthing, causing the above-noted symptoms for weeks and months after birth. Second, symptoms may appear due to an imbalance in the pancreas enzymes, which are necessary for digestion.

MASSAGE down front of thigh, deeply.

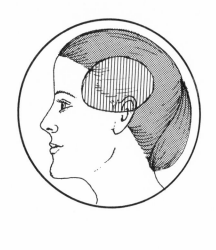
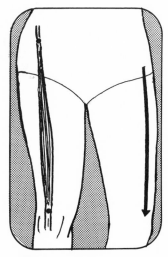

PROBLEM: Headache under the eyes. "Sinus" and cheek-bone pains. Allergy to beets.

EMOTIONAL VITAMIN: *SELF-CONTROL, USEFUL.*

NUTRITION: B-3 (niacin), B-6, false Solomon's seal.

CAUSE: An insufficient blood supply to the cheekbone area, causing toxins to build up and pain to occur.

MASSAGE up very deeply in the low back area.

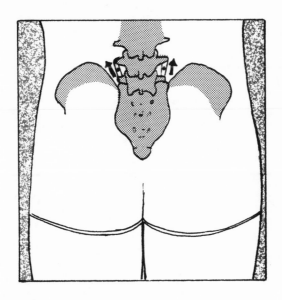

PROBLEM: Stopped-up eustachian tubes. Ears popping. Headache near the bridge of the nose. Allergy to wheat, citrus, milk products, C complex, calcium, lecithin. Tender first molar.

EMOTIONAL VITAMIN: *GOODNESS, RESPECTED.*

NUTRITION: F, teething, nerve, heal all.

CAUSE: The allergies (caused by an imbalance of the stomach and pancreas in this case), cause an excessive amount of mucus, especially near the opening of the eustachian tubes, causing them to become clogged.

MASSAGE outward and forward on the entire low back area, deeply.

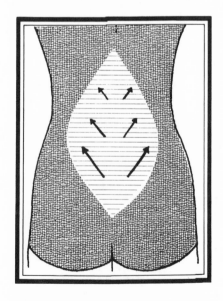

PROBLEM: Tendency to hemorrhage. Allergy to most green vegetables and bananas.

EMOTIONAL VITAMIN: *MILDNESS, HOPE.*

NUTRITION: B-2, B-6, F (linoleic acid), iron, lecithin, magnesium, mineral complex, PABA, protein powder, ferrum phos, kali phos, silicea, cayenne, Oregon grape, papaya seeds.

CAUSE: This problem generally has a series of symptoms caused by inability to properly digest certain nutrients. This causes a tendency to bleed because there is not enough vitamin K in the body for coagulation to take place.

MASSAGE the bottom of the foot from the outside near the heel toward the big toe.

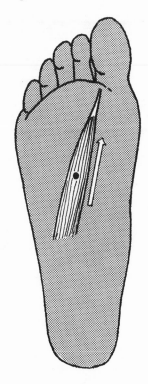

PROBLEM: Hip bone (ilium) ache. Low back ache.

EMOTIONAL VITAMIN: *FAITH, LOVED.*

NUTRITION: B-6, PABA, pancreatin complex, zinc, onion, red clover, sword fern.

CAUSE: Insufficient blood flow into the hip bone, which causes all muscles of the hip and low back to also begin to ache.

MASSAGE bottom of foot deeply from heel to little toe.

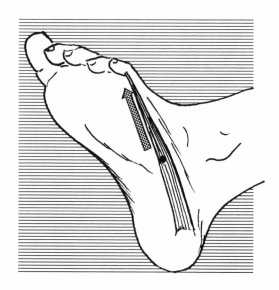

PROBLEM: Mild hypoglycemia. Dizziness. Irritability when missing meals.

EMOTIONAL VITAMIN: *PEACE, LOYAL.*

NUTRITION: E complex, lecithin, kali phos, nerve, butter.

CAUSE: This kidney and spleen problem sets off a chain reaction that causes the pancreas blood sugar level to drop enough to experience mild hypoglycemia.

MASSAGE down the forearm very deeply.

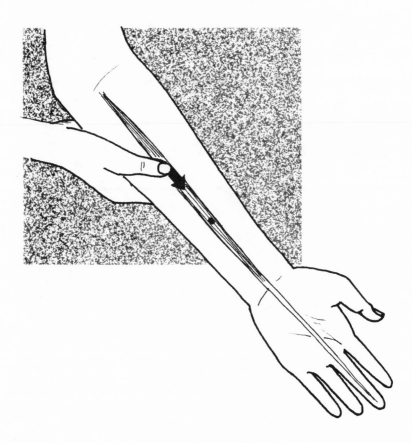

PROBLEM: Extreme weakening, fatigue, dizziness. If unusually severe, may collapse into a coma. Allergy to B-5 (pantothenic acid).

EMOTIONAL VITAMIN: *FAITH, SUCCESSFUL.*

NUTRITION: F, kelp, lecithin, mineral complex, azuki beans, chia seeds, soy protein powder.

CAUSE: This particular type of hypoglycemia (low blood sugar) is noted for its symptom of extreme weakness and faint feeling, caused by a heavy deficiency of blood sugar to the arms, legs, and brain.

MASSAGE up from the bellybutton to breastbone, and down on back of upper arm.

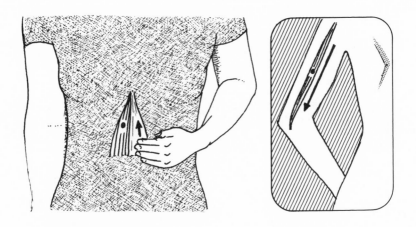

PROBLEM: Slight weakness or mild fatigue. Craving for sweets and alcohol.

EMOTIONAL VITAMIN: *MILD, FULFILLED.*

NUTRITION: B-12.

CAUSE: This form of mild hypoglycemia is caused by difficulty of balancing the blood sugar (glucose) level in storage in the liver. It is characterized by the craving for sweets or alcohol.

MASSAGE up back side of neck very deeply, and down front of lower arm.

PROBLEM: Heartburn. Feeling of fullness. Acid regurgitation. Tender tooth (1st incisor upper).

EMOTIONAL VITAMIN: *KINDNESS, SUBMISSIVE.*

NUTRITION: B-2, mineral complex, papaya.

CAUSE: These emotions assist in controlling the cardiac valve of the stomach. When this valve is imbalanced, food can come back up the esophagus, causing heartburn.

MASSAGE deeply into buttocks, pressing down and outward.

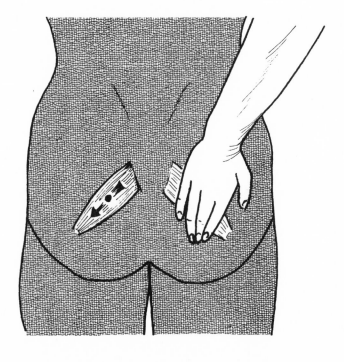

PROBLEM: Gas pains shortly after eating. Swelling and gas in the upper abdomen area (stomach) just under the breast bone. Slight headache in the temples just above the ears. Allergy to PABA.

EMOTIONAL VITAMIN: *SELF-CONTROL, FORGIVE-NESS.*

NUTRITION: B-3 (niacin), lecithin, pancreatin complex, plumb met, silicea, chicory root.

CAUSE: A forcing open of the pyloric valve of the stomach, permitting uncontrolled digestion, fermentation, and acid build-up in the small intestines.

MASSAGE upward and outward from lower back to shoulders.

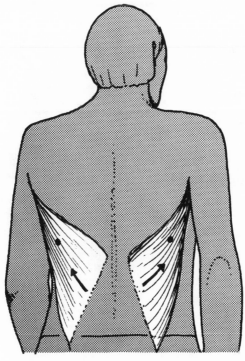

PROBLEM: Toxic reaction to insect bites and stings, such as bees, yellow jackets, hornets, mosquitoes, mites, ants, etc. Allergy to poison oak infections and watermelon.

EMOTIONAL VITAMIN: *KINDNESS, SUPPORTIVE.*

NUTRITION: B-12, lecithin, mineral complex, okra, soybeans, soy oil, soy protein powder, zinc.

CAUSE: This special hormone imbalance can be serious. It prevents your body from properly dealing with mild poisons by simply antidoting them--instead, a strong reaction occurs.

MASSAGE down the lower ¼ of the lower leg on the outside.

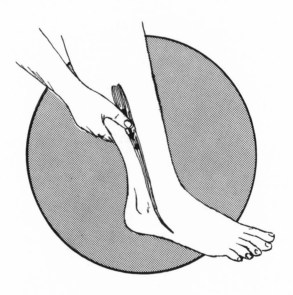

PROBLEM: Pain in the jawbone when biting. Temporo-mandibular joint syndrome.

EMOTIONAL VITAMIN: *HOPE, WANTED.*

NUTRITION: Zinc, yohimbe.

CAUSE: Stagnation of blood and lymph in the bone marrow of the jawbone.

MASSAGE up on sides of nose, and out deeply on the buttocks.

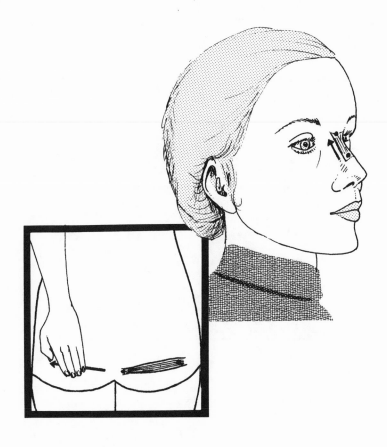

PROBLEM: Light bothers eyes. Need to wear sunglasses when outside. Mild headaches behind bridge of nose.

EMOTIONAL VITAMIN: *MILDNESS, SATISFIED.*

NUTRITION: B-2, B-3, B-6, F (linoleic acid).

CAUSE: An imbalance of the adrenal hormone that controls the dilation and contraction of the eye. It is better (and cheaper) to fix this problem than to put on harmful colored glasses!

MASSAGE out on bottom ribs, up on low belly, and in on bottom of eyes.

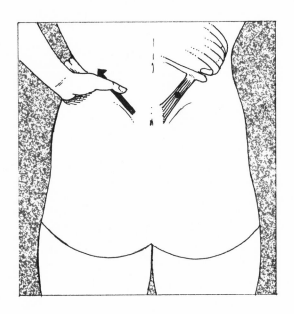

PROBLEM: Low back or sacral pains. Stiff back. Allergy to eggs, figs, and olive oil.

EMOTIONAL VITAMIN: *SELF-CONTROL, TRANQUIL.*

NUTRITION: PABA, zinc, kali phos, nat sulph, cascara sagrada.

CAUSE: Blood stagnation in low back (sacrum).

MASSAGE up and in deeply in low back area.

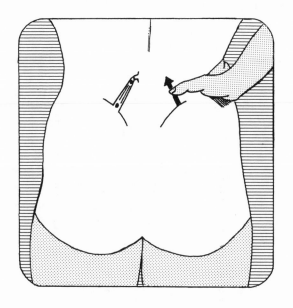

PROBLEM: Periods irregular and painful. Menopause imbalance. Tenderness and poor circulation of blood in the lateral chest area.

EMOTIONAL VITAMIN: *FAITH, SATISFIED.*

NUTRITION: E complex, lecithin, PABA, zinc, changease (Dr. Christopher's combination), homeopathic calms, nerve, teething.

CAUSE: This thyroid, pituitary, and pineal malfunction produces an imbalance in the hormones regulating menstruation and the blood supply into the sides of the chest and reproductive organs.

MASSAGE from the wrist down the palm toward the thumb, deeply.

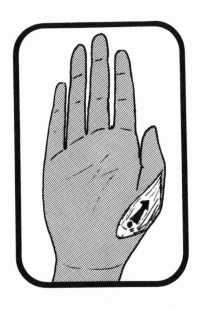

PROBLEM: Morning sickness, tilted uterus, and other problems related to pregnancy.

EMOTIONAL VITAMIN: *LONG-SUFFERING, SOCIABLE.*

NUTRITION: E plus, lecithin.

CAUSE: When this special emotional program gives out, the hypothalamus, posterior pituitary and kidney malfunction in a very small way. This leads to an imbalance in hormones that control and cause nausea. It is often brought about by a stretching movement of the uterus.

MASSAGE very deeply into the uterus area with great care and gentleness. If in doubt, go see a doctor or other professional who knows how to muscle test. It is also often helpful to sit on your heel or a small ball.

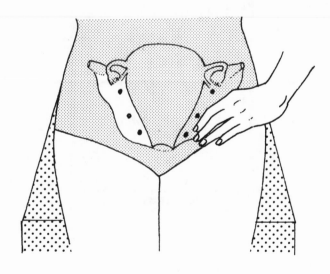

PROBLEM: Mosquitoes love you!

EMOTIONAL VITAMIN: *MILDNESS, GRATEFUL.*

NUTRITION: B-1, pepsin.

CAUSE: Imbalance of pepsin and B-1 in pancreas, creating an attractive odor for mosquitoes and other insects.

MASSAGE up back of neck.

PROBLEM: Ovary or uterus pains. Cysts in the reproductive organs. Sore lower lobe of the liver. Cysts in various organs.

EMOTIONAL VITAMIN: *FAITH, ACCEPTED.*

NUTRITION: B-6, E complex, lecithin, mineral complex, pancreatin complex, yellow dock.

CAUSE: This emotional imbalance causes small portions of the liver, pancreas, and thymus to work incorrectly. Toxins build up and often show up in the reproductive organs as cysts.

MASSAGE the upper part of the external ear toward the center.

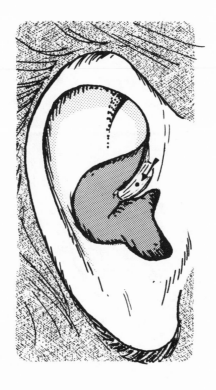

PROBLEM: Overweight problems in skin of upper abdomen. Frontal headache. Weak, tender, or clicking jaw. Pain in arch of foot. Cramping in back of lower leg when eating many bananas. Dentin becoming porous.

EMOTIONAL VITAMIN: *PEACEFULNESS, USEFULNESS.*

NUTRITION: PABA, calc flour, calc sulph, ferrum phos, kali mur, nat mur, silicea, bach flower remedies, oak and cherry plum, tiger lily.

CAUSE: Thyroid-kidney imbalance, causing a water-retention problem.

MASSAGE down outside and back of leg.

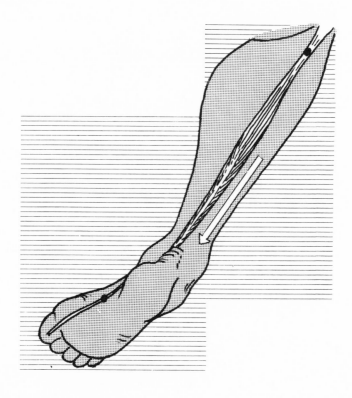

PROBLEM: Overweight. Sore outer ear. Irritation on toes and toenails.

EMOTIONAL VITAMIN: *GOODNESS, UNITED.*

NUTRITION: B-1, PABA, mag phos, garlic.

CAUSE: Not overeating, but an accumulation of too much fluid in the fatty (adipose) tissue.

MASSAGE ear thoroughly, pressing inward.

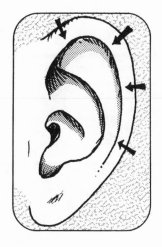

PROBLEM: Allergy to poison oak.

EMOTIONAL VITAMIN: *KIND, REMEMBERING.*

NUTRITION: B-6, lecithin, mineral complex, apple cider vinegar, ginger, popcorn.

CAUSE: The body's inability to cope with the irritant from the poison oak bush.

MASSAGE from the breast backward toward the bottom of the shoulder blade.

PROBLEM: Poison oak infection. Bladder infection. Itching of infections.

EMOTIONAL VITAMIN: *SELF-CONTROL, ADAPTABLE.*

NUTRITION: B-1, lecithin, magnesium, pancreatin complex, nat sulph, rhus tox, poison oak homeopathic.

CAUSE: Difficulty of body in combatting certain types of infections.

MASSAGE up on abdomen from navel to ribs.

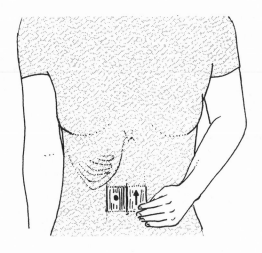

PROBLEM: Poison oak. Itchy, blistering skin.

EMOTIONAL VITAMIN: *GOODNESS, AGREEABLENESS.*

NUTRITION: Alfalfa, B-3 (niacin), B-12, iron, C complex, calcium, E complex, mineral complex, manganese, potassium-iodine, nat phos, witch hazel.

CAUSE: This is a secondary reaction to the infectious fluid produced by poison oak blisters. Use this lesson after catching poison oak.

MASSAGE deeply into buttocks pressing outward.

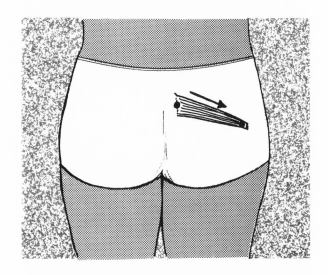

PROBLEM: Pain in area along sides of upper groin (along edge of pubic hair). This may be especially noted during the last trimester of pregnancy. Pain in groin when lifting up one leg while lying on back. Gas. Indigestion.

EMOTIONAL VITAMIN: *SELF-CONTROL, WORTHY.*

NUTRITION: Mineral complex, pancreatin complex, chamomile, lambsquarters.

CAUSE: A weakening of a large ligament in the groin, due to emotions and heavy stress by the baby's weight. Also, the pyloric valve is forced open, causing indigestion.

MASSAGE down the fold of the leg (groin) from the hip to the pubic bone.

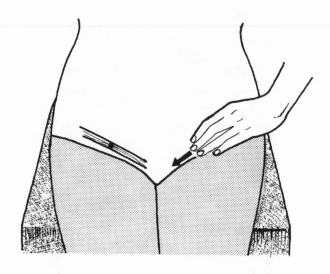

PROBLEM: Protein in urine, albuminuria. Allergy to soya products, cotton and light. "Cold syndrome," runny nose and sneezing.

EMOTIONAL VITAMIN: *WILLING, BOLD*

NUTRITION: A, B-6, C complex, garlic and parsley, mineral complex, yarrow. Possible additions: niacin, lecithin, herbal diuretic, nat mur.

CAUSE: A breakdown in the hormone/enzyme interconnection between the adrenal medulla, anterior pituitary and pancreas, causes the body to throw protein into the urine. This is especially true during pregnancy because of the stress of a pelvic muscle involved.

MASSAGE down deeply on your shoulder muscles.

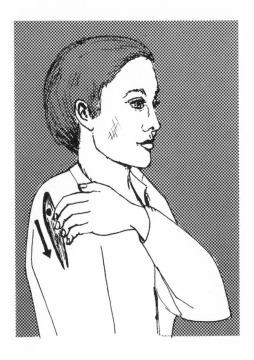

PROBLEM: Itchy, scaly knees (housemaid's knees) and elbows.

EMOTIONAL VITAMIN: *MILDNESS, HUMBLE.*

NUTRITION: Pancreatin, columbine, lobelia, strawberry leaves.

CAUSE: A hormone imbalance between the liver, gallbladder, and adrenals, which causes the skin to grow improperly at the elbows and knees.

MASSAGE deeply on your buttocks from center toward the hip joint.

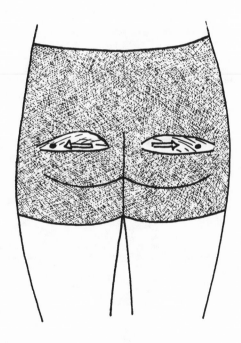

PROBLEM: Itchy, scaly knees and elbows. Pains in the elbow joint.

EMOTIONAL VITAMIN: *MILDNESS, UNDERSTANDING.*

NUTRITION: Pancreatin, columbine, lobelia, strawberry leaves.

CAUSE: A hormone imbalance between the liver, gallbladder, and adrenals, which causes the skin to grow improperly at the elbows and knees.

MASSAGE down the outside of the lower end of the upper arm, all the way to your wrist on the palm side.

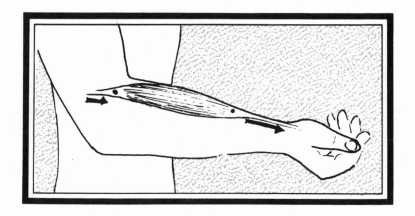

PROBLEM: Burning, shooting pains on the insides of the upper legs and outside of the lower legs. Low neck pains.

EMOTIONAL VITAMIN: *GOODNESS, FAITH.*

NUTRITION: C complex, E complex, mineral complex, soy protein powder, golden seal, red clover, lobelia.

CAUSE: A pinching of the sciatic nerve in the low back area.

MASSAGE very gently and deeply into the low abdomen and up the back, near the bottom of the ribs.

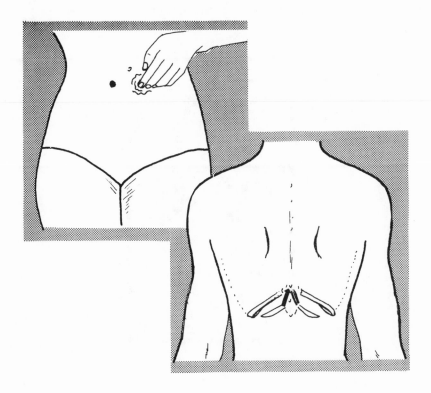

PROBLEM: Sore throat in back of mouth. Dry cough. Allergy to polyester. Irregular ovulation or menstrual period or spotting.

EMOTIONAL VITAMIN: *SELF-CONTROL, COURAGE.*

NUTRITION: Lecithin, mineral complex.

CAUSE. A nerve response to the anterior pituitary and thyroid is malsignaling, causing a lack of blood flow to the upper throat and an imbalance in hormone secretions, affecting the ovulation cycle.

MASSAGE by vibrating deeply up under jaw and from the middle of the breastbone toward the shoulder.

PROBLEM: Sore throat "down deep," in the esophagus. Difficulty in swallowing. Allergy to honey, figs, and raisins.

EMOTIONAL VITAMIN: *SELF-CONTROL, UNDERSTOOD*

NUTRITION: E complex, maple syrup.

CAUSE: Throat (esophagus) muscles and surrounding tissues used for swallowing are not receiving sufficient lymph circulation, causing swelling and soreness.

MASSAGE all of the throat area, *gently*, in small circles.

PROBLEM: Sore throat below the Adam's apple. Vaginal irritations. Yeast infections. Canker sores. Congestion in the small intestines.

EMOTIONAL VITAMIN: *GOODNESS, UNDERSTOOD.*

NUTRITION: Calcium, PABA.

CAUSE: This nerve irritation is first seen in the lower throat, causing a sore throat. Sometimes this imbalance is severe enough to cause unhealthy tissue in the vagina, giving rise to several types of infection.

MASSAGE in the midthroat area with a vibrating motion, and then down on the side of the leg above the knee.

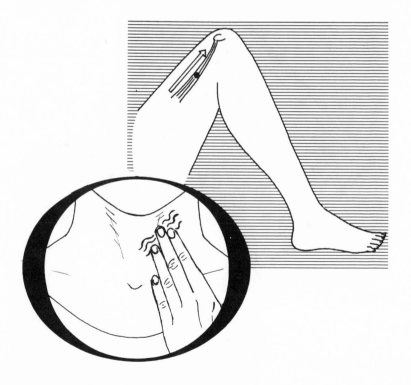

PROBLEM: Sore upper throat. Thrush. Allergy to honey, figs, raisins, bananas, apricots.

EMOTIONAL VITAMIN: *MILD, COURAGE.*

NUTRITION: Pancreatin complex, zinc, slippery elm.

CAUSE: A lack of proper lymph and blood supply to the upper throat area, causing unhealthy tissue that can be infected easily.

MASSAGE by vibrating deeply up under jaw.

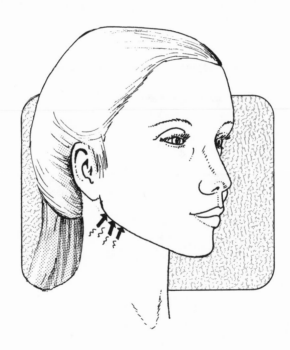

PROBLEM: Bright light bothers eyes, causing squinting. Photophobia. Sneezing when entering into direct sunlight. Dry cheeks. Need to wear sunglasses. Allergy to honey, molasses, and mustard greens.

EMOTIONAL VITAMIN: *SELF-CONTROL, SATISFIED.*

NUTRITION: B-2, ponderosa needles.

CAUSE: Imbalance of the adrenal hormone, which controls the dilation and contraction of the eye (iris). This causes one to become overly sensitive to sunlight.

MASSAGE by pressing up under back of inner anklebone.

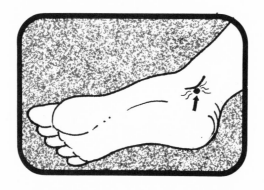

PROBLEM: Tennis elbow (elbow and wrist pains). Pain in first premolar.

EMOTIONAL VITAMIN: *JOYFUL, GRATEFUL.*

NUTRITION: F, PABA.

CAUSE: This emotion weakens a strong muscle that assists in holding the elbow and wrist joints together. Weakness causes malalignment and incorrect wear on the joints—pain!

MASSAGE down the arm, starting from the outside of the arm just above the elbow to halfway down the arm on the front, toward the little finger.

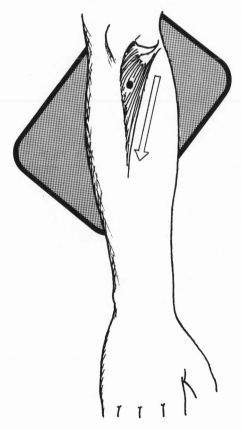

PROBLEM: Tennis elbow. Pains in the wrist and elbow joints. Carpal tunnel syndrome.

EMOTIONAL VITAMIN: *MILDNESS, ACCEPTED.*

NUTRITION: B-6, B-12, C complex, F, mineral complex, teething, soy protein powder, slippery elm.

CAUSE: This malfunction of emotions can cause a wrist muscle to weaken and the wrist and elbow joints to move incorrectly—causing pains.

MASSAGE across the lower end of the arm from the little finger side to the thumb side on the front of the arm.

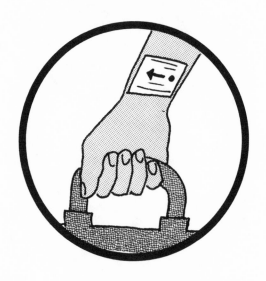

PROBLEM: Sore throat. Tonsillitis. Allergy to garlic, A, B-6, Iron.

EMOTIONAL VITAMIN: *KINDNESS, BRAVE, COOPERATIVE.*

NUTRITION: B-12, zinc, nat phos.

CAUSE: An imbalance of nerve supply to the tonsils, predisposing them to infection.

MASSAGE out on bottom of ribs in back.

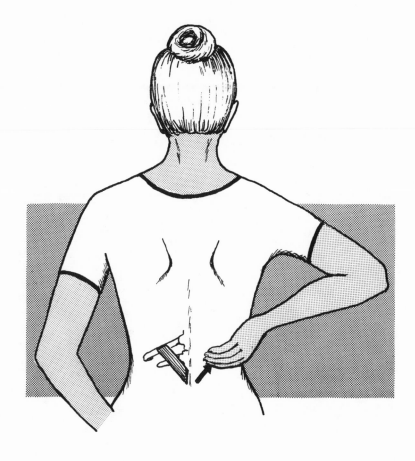

PROBLEM: Irritated, itchy vagina. Knee pains.

EMOTIONAL VITAMIN: *GOODNESS, LISTENING.*

NUTRITION: Calcium, PABA.

CAUSE: An imbalance of adrenal and thyroid hormones, causing an unhealthy vagina.

MASSAGE down on lower half of upper leg on the outside.

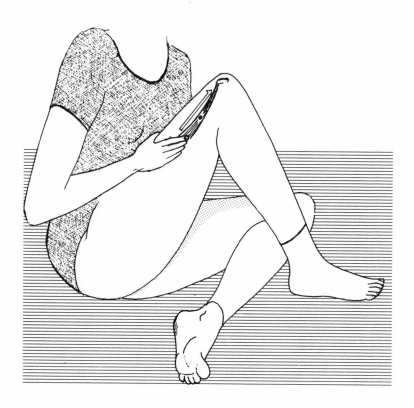

Appendix

MUSCLE-ORGAN INVOLVEMENT

It will be noted that in each problem (symptom) listed, we gave you emotions, nutrition, other symptoms, and locations to massage. Most of the locations to massage (and test) are muscles, tendons, or ligaments that are directly involved in the symptoms by relationship through the nervous, blood circulatory or lymphatic circulatory systems. There is also a direct connection to any of various series of organ reactions. For those of you wishing to pursue this field further, we have included the following list:

#	TISSUE	ORGAN
1.	GASTROCNEMIUS MEDIAL HEAD CENTRAL	ANTERIOR PITUITARY
2.	INTERTRANSVERSARRI ANTERIOR T5	ADRENAL MEDULLA
3.	SEMISPINALIS CAPITIS T1 TENDON	THYMUS
4.	SPHINCTER URETHRAE MEMBRANE #1	HEART
5.	SPHINCTER URETHRAE MEMBRANE #3	THYMUS
6.	BRACHIALIS TENDON	SMALL INTESTINE
7.	ILIO-LUMBAR LIGAMENT	POSTERIOR PITUITARY

#	TISSUE	ORGAN
8.	LONGISSIMUS CERVICIS T4	POSTERIOR PITUITARY
9.	BRACHIALIS LATERAL TENDON	PANCREAS
10.	FLEXOR DIGITORUM SUBLIMIS MIDDLE FINGER LATERAL	LIVER
11.	SCALENUS MEDIUS C1 TENDON	PANCREAS
12.	LONGUS COLLI VERTICAL C7	SMALL INTESTINE
13.	BRACHIORADIALIS MEDIAL	STOMACH
14.	FLEXOR DIGITORUM BREVIS 3rd. TOE LATERAL TENDON	ADRENAL MEDULLA
15.	ILIACUS MAJOR	EYE
16.	QUADRATUS LABII INFERIOR	SPLEEN
17.	LONGUS COLLI INFERIOR OBLIQUE T1	STOMACH CARDIAC VALVE
18.	QUADRATUS LUMBORUM #3 TENDON	BREAST
19.	PLANTAR APONEUROSIS OF FOOT CENTRAL PORTION	ADRENAL CORTEX
20.	ADDUCTOR HALLUCIS TRANS- VERSE HEAD METATARSAL 4	PANCREAS ENZYMES
21.	SALPINGOPHRYNGEUS	THYROID
22.	FLEXOR HALLUCIS LONGUS	OVARIES, TESTES
23.	TENSOR FASCIA LATA TENDON	RECTUM
24.	ROTATOR BREVIS T4	ADRENAL MEDULLA
25.	LONGUS CAPITIS C5	POSTERIOR PITUITARY
26.	LONGISSIMUS CERVICIS T1	EYE

#	TISSUE	ORGAN
27.	RECTUS CAPITIŚ POSTERIOR MINOR	THYMUS
28.	BUCCINATOR SUPERIOR INFERIOR, OPPONENS POLLICIS #2	THYMUS SKIN
29.	LONGUS COLLI VERTICAL C6	SMALL INTESTINE
30.	SCALENUS MEDIUS C5	THYMUS
31.	AURICULARIS SUPERIOR	LUNGS
32.	COCCYGEUS EXTENSOR	PINEAL
33.	BULBOCAVERNOSUS TENDON	PANCREAS ENZYME
34.	INTERTRANSVERSARII POSTERIOR	SPLEEN
35.	LUMBAR FASCIA #2	BREAST
36.	ADDUCTOR HALLUCIS OBLIQUE HEAD METATARSAL #4	PANCREAS ENZYME
37.	ABDUCTOR DIGITI QUINTI MEDIAL OF FOOT	HEART
38.	FLEXOR DIGITORUM PROFUNDUS MIDDLE FINGER	KIDNEY
39.	RECTUS ABDOMINIS #5	HYPOTHALAMUS
40.	SCALENUS POSTERIOR C5	PINEAL
41.	GLUTEUS MAXIMUS DEEP	STOMACH CARDIAC VALVE
42.	LATISSIMUS DORSI	HEART
43.	PERONEUS TERTIUS	EAR
44.	PROCERUS #1 TENDON OBTURATOR EXTERNUS TENDON	HYPOTHALAMUS PINEAL

#	TISSUE	ORGAN
45.	SERRATUS POSTERIOR INFERIOR #4	ADRENAL MEDULLA
46.	QUADRATUS LUMBORUM #4 TENDON	ADRENAL CORTEX
47.	ABDUCTOR POLLICIC BREVIS RADIAL HEAD	THYROID
48.	BROAD LIGAMENT OF UTERUS	HYPOTHALAMUS
49.	SEMISPINALIS CAPITIS C7	PANCREAS ENZYME
50.	HELICIS MINOR	THYMUS
51.	FLEXOR HALLUCIS LONGUS TENDON	URINARY BLADDER
52.	AURICULAR CARTILAGE (PINNA)	SIGMOID COLON
53.	SERRATUS ANTERIOR #9 TENDON	THYMUS
54.	RECTUS ABDOMINIS #4	THYMUS
55.	PIRIFORMIS TENDON #4	POSTERIOR PITUITARY
56.	POUPART'S LIGAMENT	THYROID
57.	DELTOID SUPERIOR POSTERIOR	URINARY BLADDER
58.	GEMELLUS SUPERIOR TENDON	GALLBLADDER
59.	BRACHIORADIALIS MEDIAL TENDON	LIVER
60.	INTERTRANSVERSARII ANTERIOR L5, MULTIFIDUS DEEP T12	LIVER GALLBLADDER
61.	CONSTRICTOR OF PHARYNX SUPERIOR #2 PECTORALIS MINOR MEDIAL	THYROID PROSTRATE- -UTERUS

#	TISSUE	ORGAN
62.	ESOPHAGUS LONGITUDINAL	PROSTRATE-UTERUS
63.	CONSTRICTOR OF PHARYNX INFERIOR, ARTICULARIS GENUS LATERAL	PROSTATE-UTERUS THYROID
64.	CONSTRUCTOR OF PHARYNX SUPERIOR #1	THYROID
65.	INTEROSSEOUS TALO-CALCANEAN LIGAMENT	ADRENAL MEDULLA
66.	ANCONEUS	PANCREAS ENZYME
67.	PRONATOR QUADRATUS	PANCREAS BLOOD SUGAR
68.	SERRATUS POSTERIOR INFERIOR #3	SMALL INTESTINE
69.	ARTICULARIS GENUS LATERAL	THYROID

Is this list complete? Is this all there is to health? By no means. This partial list of muscles, organs and their previously-related symptoms of imbalance are only a beginning. Other books published by the BIO-KINESIOLOGY INSTITUTE cover many more problems and solutions.

Note: For those muscles difficult to massage, we have given their antagonists. See the book *Quick Ready Reference.*

BIBLIOGRAPHY

A Barefoot Doctor's Manual, U. S. Dept. of Health and Welfare.

A Course in Manipulative Therapy, Dr. Randolph Stone.

Aid to Bible Understanding, Watchtower.

Allergies—How to Find and Conquer, Biokinesiology Institute.

Applied Kinesiology, David S. Walther.

Applied Kinesiology Research Manuals, George Goodheart.

Awake! Magazine, Watchtower.

Be Your Own Chiropractor, Biokinesiology Institute (Barton).

Behavioral Kinesiology, John Diamond.

How to Take Care of Yourself Naturally, Biokinesiology Institute (Barton).

Making Your Family Life Happy, Watchtower.

M. R. T., Dr. Walter Fichman and Dr. Mark Grinims.

Rolfing, Ida Rolf.

Shiatsu Therapy, Toru Namikoshi.

The Eclectic Approach to Chiropractic, Fred Stoner.

Touch for Health, John Thie.

Index

Poison oak, 68, 78, 79, 80
Psoriasis, 46

R

Repetition, 17
Rules, 9, 13

S

Sacrum, 58, 71
Scalp, itchy, 50
Scaly knees and elbows, 83, 84
Sciatica, 85
Shoulders stiff, 51
Skin rash, 38, 52, 54
Small intestine, 26, 88
Sneezing, 82, 90
Snowballing emotions, 21, 22
Solomon, 1
Sore throat, 86, 87, 88, 89, 93
Stings, 68
Stress, physical, 24
Sunglasses, 70, 90
Swallowing, 87
Sweets, 65
Symptoms, 7, 23
Synthetics, 9

T

Tailbone, 57, 58
Teeth, 29, 31, 48, 55, 60, 66, 76, 91
Temporo-Mandibular-Joint (T.M.J.), 69
Tennis elbow, 91, 92

Testing:
  concept, 8
  emotional, 13, 14
  example, 18
  locations, 11
  rules, 9, 10, 11
Thrush, 89
Tissue, abnormal, 47
Toes, 77
Tonsillitis, 93
Touch testing, 9, 10, 11, 18
Toxic reaction to insects, 67
Transverse colon, 27
Tumors, 46

U

Uterus, 73, 74

V

Vagina, 29, 88, 94
Varicose veins, 35, 36
Verify nutrition, 11, 12
Vomiting—See Acid regurgitation

W

Walking difficulty, 40
Warning, iv
Weakness, 64
"Worry-wart," 47
Wrist, 9, 10, 91, 92
Wrong vitamin, 4

Y

Yeast infection, 88, 94
Yellow jacket, 68

PRINCIPLED & UNIQUE

BE YOUR OWN CHIROPRACTOR

The gentle way to structural alignment. Learn how to help yourself and your family to feel better.

Do you continually have particular muscles that are sore or tight? When you are tired, do you notice a specific part of your body giving out?

This book is the first of its kind that shows you WHY and WHAT to do! Learn to make corrections that strengthen the emotions, their specific organs and muscles all at one time. Explanations and photos of tension-releasing exercises for young and old. Cost: $10.00. 200 pages.

WHICH VITAMIN, WHICH HERB DO I NEED?

A book designed for home use in all aspects of nutritional care.

With much practice and determined effort you can learn the art of specific muscle testing, a way to use your own body and mind to determine your individual needs. MAKE SURE you are buying high quality food that is good for YOU as an individual! 64 pages. Cost: $2.00.

HOW TO TAKE CARE OF YOURSELVES NATURALLY

A manual to lead you to better health. It presents Muscle Testing (Biokinesiology) as a superb tool in the successful unity of many therapies. Chocked-full of research into nutrition, reflexology, mind/body responses, colors, allergy testing, and a surprising new method of massage therapy. 160 pages. Cost: $8.00.

ALLERGIES--HOW TO FIND AND CONQUER!

A practical reference and "how to" book listing over 100 specific allergies and their EMOTIONAL-NUTRITIONAL-STRUCTURAL interrelationships. From ACRILYCS to ZINC. A valuable aid for the instructor and the family. 270 pages, heavily illustrated. Cost: $15.00

BOOKS THAT DO NOT⌐

QUICK READY REFERENCE

Are you ready to expand your muscle testing, your energy balancing? Here is the reference book that begins to open a broad, new field for the Applied Kinesiologist. It lists EMOTIONS, NUTRITION, STRUCTURE, and ANTAGONIST information on 815 muscles, tendons, ligaments, synovial membranes, fascias, and intervertebral discs. 300 pages of useful information for the instructor—the professional. Limited edition. Cost: $25.00.

THE ATLAS

An outstanding reference book! The ATLAS has 815 full-page pictures of the individual muscles, tendons, ligaments, fascias and synovial membranes. It lists the following information for each tissue: organ, LAN system (one of 20 acupressure meridians), emotions, secondary other tissues involved (such as skin, bones, teeth, nerve plexuses, etc.), nutrition, antagonist, symptoms, origin, insertion, massage direction, action, cranial nerve, method of testing and biokinetic exercise. 100 pages of in-depth indexes and cross-references: standard symptoms, bones, teeth, circulatory systems, etc. This book is for the professional. If you have it—you'll use it! Cost: $100.00.

ORGAN/EMOTION CHART

Detailed wall chart, 35" x 24". It clearly shows 87 important areas for "Therapy Localization," such as: organs, LANs (similar to neurovasculars) and other tissues. AND—the POSITIVE STRENGTHENING EMOTIONS for each point! Cost: $5.00 (add $2.00 postage for each order of charts).

GATHER DUST!

BIOKINESIOLOGY
Touchstone of Holistic Health

CREATIVE HEALTH NEWSLETTER

Have you ever wondered what you can do about: diaper rash? wheat grass allergy? air pollution? purchasing the correct vitamins and herbs? low back aches?

The Newsletter covers these and many more topics of interest to families and professionals. Printed once every two months. Cost: $10.00 USA; $12.00 Canada; $14.00 for other countries per year.

Qty	Cost	Total	Publication
_____	$10	_____	Be Your Own Chiropractor
_____	$ 2	_____	Which Vitamin, Which Herb?
_____	$ 8	_____	How to Take Care of Yourselves Naturally
_____	$10	_____	Creative Health Newsletter
_____	$15	_____	Allergies—How to Find and Conquer
_____	$25	_____	Quick Ready Reference
_____	$100	_____	The Atlas
_____	$5 + $2	_____	Emotion/Organ Chart ($2.00 postage)
_____	$10	_____	Biokinesiology Vol. II
_____	$5.95	_____	Muscle Testing
	$1		Postage $1.00 per order
_____	_____	_____	**TOTAL: ALL ORDERS MUST BE PREPAID**

Prices subject to change.

_____ Information on Biokinesiology Classes

_____ Information on Cooper's Minerals, Herbs, and Vitamins

Name _____ Phone _____

Address _____

City _____ State _____ Zip _____

Send to: BIOKINESIOLOGY INSTITUTE
  461 Sawyer Rd.
  Shady Cove, OR 97539 U.S.A.
  Phone: (503) 878-2398 or 878-2080